R'S LICENSE

OUSINE COMMISSION

2017

IGMUND

License Number

23841

W9-CNE-916

TAXI DRIVER WISDOM

BY **RISA MICKENBERG**
PHOTOGRAPHY **JOANNE DUGAN**
DESIGN **BRIAN LEE HUGHES**

CHRONICLE BOOKS
SAN FRANCISCO

This Chronicle Books LLC edition published in 2016.
Introduction copyright © 2016 Risa Mickenberg
Copyright © 1996 by Risa Mickenberg
Photographs copyright © 1996 by Joanne Dugan

ISBN: 978-1-4521-5763-4

The Library of Congress has cataloged the original edition as follows:

Taxi Driver Wisdom / [collected by] Risa Mckenbert :
 photographs by Joanne Dugan
p.   cm.
ISBN 0-8118-1165-4
1. Quotations. English. 2. American with and humor.
I. Mickenberg, Risa. II. Dugan, Joanne.
PN6081.T28 1995
081--dc20   95-22085
                                       CIP

Manufactured in China.

This edition typeset by John Parise

10 9 8 7 6 5 4 3 2 1

Chronicle Books LLC
680 Second Street
San Francisco, California 94107
www.chroniclebooks.com

<u>ALL THE QUOTES IN THIS BOOK WERE TAKEN FROM</u> <u>CONVERSATIONS WITH NEW YORK CITY CAB DRIVERS.</u>

THANK YOU:

Abdul, Abdul, Achileas, Ahmed, Aitzaz, Anitoliy, Angel, Aqueel, Augustin, Belgaam, Ben, Bernard, Bolivar, Carlos, David, Dilawar, Eamon, Edouard, Feliks, Fils Jean, Francisco, Garri, Gladys, Gurmeet, Hafiz, Hanif, Hardial, Hassan, Humayun, Igor, Ishrat, Jaime, James, Jamil, Jaspal, Jean, Jean, Jean, Jean, Jean Fils, Jesus, Jitendev, John, Kahled, Kahlil, Karnail, Kofi, Lawrence, Leocadio, Leonel, Leslie, Libardo, Louis, Maamar, Mahlik, Malid, Mauricio, Michael, Mieczyslow, Mohinder, Muhamed, Muhammed, Muhammed, Muhammed, Munawar, Nelson, Omar, Oomen, Peter, Philip, Philip, Pushap, Ramen, Ramon, Ramon, Rene, Richard, Rousseau, Sahik, Sainristal, Salimm, Sam, Samir, Serge, Shawsul, Sheldon, Sidi, Silvio, Staphano, Sukwinder, Tahir, Taujeed, Vasilios, Willince.

I think Jean-Paul Sartre picked me up outside the Knicks game last week. Or was it Krishnamurti? The truth is, most of the world's greatest philosophers wouldn't look out of place on a hack license.

New York cab drivers are the world's most accessible source of truth and wisdom. Where else can you have intimate discussions with someone from Tibet, Bangladesh, Liberia, India, Zaire, Pakistan, Vietnam, Iran, Russia, Haiti, Peru, Lithuania, Poland, the Ivory Coast?

Where else can you hear the wisdom of Taoism, Hinduism, Shintoism, Buddhism, Islam, Santeria, Zógqen, Zoroastrianism?

Maybe because people can only deal with limited-time intimacy, we get into a taxi and suddenly we can reveal our souls. We can ask questions we've been afraid to ask.

A cab is a kind of confessional-mobile. Musky with incense or air freshener, sealed off from the rest of the world, slide open that glass divider and it's just you and your guru, sharing a few minutes of reflection and advice.

An ashram costs $5,000 a week. A psychiatrist costs $250 an hour. An astrologist will run you around

$100. But a cab ride is only $2.50 for the first mile, plus fifty cents per ⅕ mile or 60 seconds in slow traffic or when the vehicle is stopped.

In cabs, I have learned how to fight fairly, how to manage fear, when to accept fate, when to avoid midtown.

The next time you're in a taxi, ask the driver what function truth serves. Ask why evil exists. Ask if jealousy contradicts love. Keep your mind and your bulletproof window open. As Ralph Waldo Emerson said, "In every man, there is something wherein I may learn of him." Or as one cabdriver put it, "If you're a smart person, you can see what's smart about the next guy. If you're secretly afraid you're a moron, okay, then, to you, everybody's a moron."

In the twenty years since this book was first published, the wisdom within remains as true as ever. And in the era of lost-without-an-app rideshare drivers, there's still no better route than with a cabbie who knows more than just where you're going.

EVERYTHING COMES OUT THE SAME, NO MATTER WHETHER YOU MAKE IT HARD ON YOURSELF OR NOT.

AS SOON AS YOU MEET SOMEONE, YOU KNOW THE REASONS WHY YOU WILL LEAVE THEM.

VIETNAM WAR IS FINISHED BUT SIXTH AVENUE CONSTRUCTION IS NEVER FINISHED.

THERE IS NO CHIVALRY. FOR THAT, YOU HAVE TO GO UPSTATE.

NEW SHOES ALWAYS HURT.

LOVE IS 90% RESPONSIBILITY. WHATEVER THAT OTHER 10 PERCENT IS, IT MUST BE QUITE SOMETHING.

I SEE MORE OF WHAT IS GOING ON AROUND ME BECAUSE I AM NOT CONCERNED WITH FINDING A PARKING PLACE.

YOU HAVE THIS ON THE ONE HAND, THAT ON THE OTHER HAND. THAT IS WHY YOU WRING YOUR HANDS.

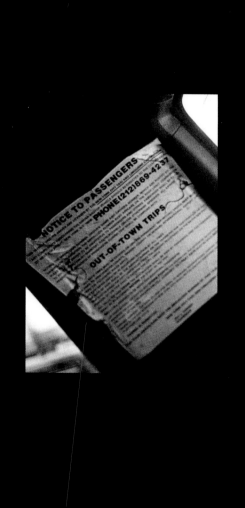

YOU'RE NOT ANY SAFER IN FIRST CLASS.

WHEN YOUR MAN IS
MAD, WAIT,
WAIT UNTIL HE'S IN
THE RIGHT MOOD.
NEVER APPROACH
FIRE WITH GAS.

THERE'S A LOT OF FISH IN THE AIR.

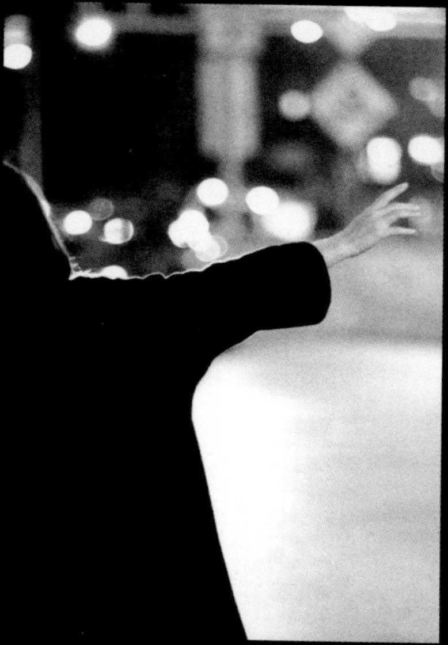

IF SOMEONE STEALS YOUR CAB, THEN IT WASN'T YOUR CAB.

AS A COUPLE GETS OLDER, THEY PLEASURE EACH OTHER WITH LAUGHTER INSTEAD OF SEX.

YOU MARRY OUT OF YOUR GREATEST LOVE OR YOUR GREATEST FEAR.

PEOPLE LOOK SO MUCH BETTER ALONE.

THE WORSE A TOWN'S ECONOMY IS, THE BETTER LOOKING THE GUYS WHO WORK AT THE LOCAL GAS STATIONS ARE.

THE MOUTH IS THE MOST DANGEROUS PART OF A PERSON.

WE STARVE EACH OTHER AND THEN WE FEAST ON EACH OTHER.

THE THINGS YOU LOVE ARE AS STUPID AS THE THINGS YOU HATE AND ARE EASILY INTERCHANGEABLE.

DON'T BE CONSERVATIVE WITH A NEW LOVE. BE LIBERAL AND YOU WILL FIND WHAT YOU WANT TO KNOW. DON'T STOP THEM AT EACH THING THEY SAY OR THEY WILL TRY TO BE CAREFUL WITH YOU AND YOU'LL NEVER KNOW WHAT SORT OF PERSON THEY WANT TO BE.

YOU SAY WHAT YOU LIKE TO HEAR.

WHEN THERE IS SOMETHING YOU WANT, IT SEEMS IT IS EVERYWHERE.

MOSTLY I JUST HATE TO SLEEP ALONE.

EACH DAY IS LIKE ANOTHER BUD ON A TREE: IMPOSSIBLE WITHOUT THE TREE BENEATH IT.

YOU CAN'T GO WITH THE PERSON WHO LOVES YOU. THAT MEANS NOTHING. YOU HAVE TO BE WITH THE PERSON WHO YOU LOVE.

I ENJOY FIREWORKS BUT STARS IS NICE TOO.

YOU CAN TAKE THE GIRL OUT OF THE CHEAP UNDERWEAR, BUT YOU CAN'T TAKE THE CHEAP UNDERWEAR OUT OF THE GIRL.

IF YOU'RE A SMART
PERSON, YOU CAN SEE
WHAT'S SMART ABOUT
THE NEXT GUY.
IF YOU'RE SECRETLY
AFRAID YOU'RE A
MORON, OKAY,
THEN TO YOU,
EVERYBODY'S A MORON.

IF YOU ARE GOOD AT ANYTHING, THAT IS BEAUTY.

PLEASE HAVE
FARE READY
WHEN REACHIN
DESTINATION

FOR A CAB DRIVER, EVERYTHING IS UPSIDE DOWN. IF A PERSON HAS $4 AND THE METER SAYS $4 AND THEY WANT TO GO A FEW MORE BLOCKS, I WILL TAKE THEM, BUT I HAVE TO SHUT MY METER AND IF I SHUT MY METER, TLC (TAXI & LIMOUSINE COMMISSION) WILL GIVE ME A TICKET FOR $100. THIS IS WHAT I MEAN ABOUT A SOCIETY THAT VALUES MONEY OVER LOVE.

YOU MUST HAVE THINGS THAT YOU CARE ABOUT. OTHERWISE YOU ARE EMPTY.

THE TRAFFIC—
IT SLOWS,
IT SPEEDS UP
AGAIN FOR
NO REASON
SOMETIMES.

IF A MAN KEEPS TELLING YOU HE LOVES YOU, OVER AND OVER, THEN SOMETHING IS WRONG.

THE CAR, IT DRIVES ITSELF. YOU JUST ASK IT TO TURN.

BIKE MESSENGERS— THEY SEARCH FOR DEATH.

NO EATING
OR DRINKING
THIS CAR

YOU HAVE NO ONE TO BLAME BUT YOURSELF AND EVERYONE HAS YOU TO BLAME, TOO.

DON'T WORRY IF
ONE PERSON IS NOT
SHOWING THE SAME
LOVE THAT SOMEONE
ELSE HAS SHOWN YOU.
NO TWO LOVES ARE
THE SAME.

TRAVEL IS TO SPREAD YOUR LIFE ALL OVER THE WORLD.

TO PREPARE
YOURSELF FOR
MARRIAGE, YOU
MUST THINK:
I AM GOING
TO BURY THIS
PERSON.

WHAT EVERYONE LIKES THE BEST IS MONEY, BUT THEY DON'T SAY IT.

IT'S ALWAYS BETTER TO BE BEHIND A POLICE CAR.

IF THERE IS UNDERSTANDING, THERE IS LOVE. IF THERE IS NO UNDERSTANDING, THERE IS ONLY AN ENDLESS STREAM OF QUESTIONS.

IF SOMEONE GETS RICH, I DO NOT CHEER FOR THEM. I WEEP FOR MYSELF.

THE RICH GUYS, THOSE ARE THE CHEAP ONES. UNLESS THEY ARE ON A DATE. A POOR MAN WHO IS WITH HIS FAMILY, HE APPRECIATES WHAT IT IS TO WORK. HE WILL BE A BIG TIPPER.

ashes to ashes

WE ARE ALL BORN POOR.

3.75

DON'T LOOK AT WHAT HE IS NOT. LOOK AT WHAT HE IS.

YOU SEE IN OTHER PEOPLE WHAT YOU WANT FOR YOURSELF.

IT'S "WHEN YOU'RE WITH ME, YOU'RE KILLING ME. WHEN YOU'RE NOT, I'M DYING."

IT'S BORING WHEN YOU LIVE BY YOURSELF.

YOU SAY YOU ARE HAPPY, YOU ARE LYING.

EVERYBODY GO DIFFERENT WAY TO SEE THE SAME THING.

THIS JEALOUSY, I HAVE SEEN IN MY SISTERS, BUT NOT IN MY BROTHERS.

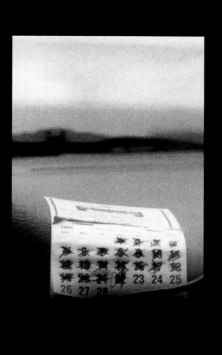

TRUST NOBODY. YOU HAVE TO GET EVERYTHING ON PAPER.

LOVE IS LIKE A WEIGHT ON A SCALE. ONE PERSON OR THE OTHER BEARS ITS BURDEN.

MEN GET SUCCESSFUL TO PREVENT OURSELVES FROM BEING HURT.

SOME PEOPLE, THEY PREFER WHEN YOU FAIL.

IF YOU CHOSE A NEW LIFE, YOU MUST HAVE NOT WANTED THE OLD ONE ANYMORE.

38, 48, 50. THESE NUMBERS ALWAYS BUSY. LOADING, UNLOADING, ALWAYS GET MESSED UP. CRAZY.

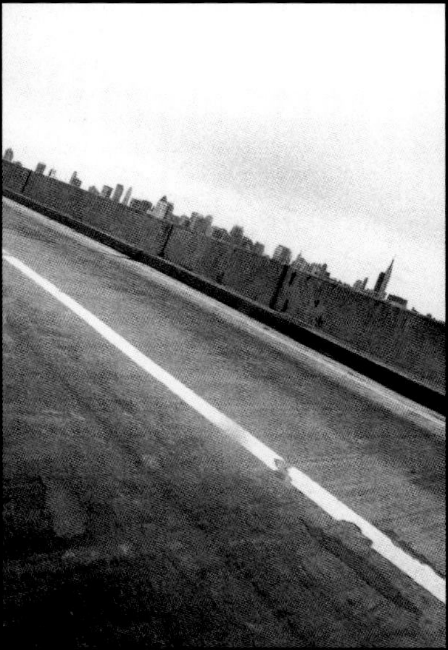

I'M FOR BETTER ALWAYS. I'M FOR FUTURE.

PLEASE PROTECT YOUR PERSON

POR FAVOR PROTEJAN SUS OBJET

POR FAVOR PROTEGGETE I VOSTRI

THERE ARE THREE MAIN RELIGIONS: JUDAISM, CHRISTIANITY, AND ISLAM, AND ALL HAVE THE STORY OF JOSEPH. WE SHARE THE SAME STORIES, BUT WE FIGHT EACH OTHER.

WE ALL CONNECT, LIKE A NET WE CANNOT SEE.

I NEVER BY ACCIDENT. I ONLY ON PURPOSE.

WE DO EVERYTHING FOR OURSELVES.

HOW DIRTY YOU CAN TALK DEPENDS ON WHICH SUMMER JOB YOU HAVE.

I LIKE DRIVING.
OTHERWISE I TAKE
ANOTHER JOB.
EACH THING CAN
BE EVERYTHING
FOR YOU.
YOU MAKE DRIVING
EVERYTHING.

ENGLAND, THAT WAS
CALLED BRITANNIA.
THEN THE JEWISH
TRIBES CAME IN AND
THEY WERE YIDDISH
AND THEY USED A LOT
OF "ISH" SO THEY
CALLED THEM BRITISH.

IF YOU ARE ALWAYS LATE, IT IS BECAUSE YOU ARE TRYING TO MAKE THE THINGS FASTER.

IT'S THE WOMEN, THEY ARE WHO ALWAYS HOLD UP THE LANGUAGES, THE TRADITIONS.

NEVER BE EMBARRASSED ABOUT SOMETHING YOU LIKE.

WHEN YOU THINK YOU HAVE LOST SOMETHING, IT IS USUALLY STILL WITH YOU.

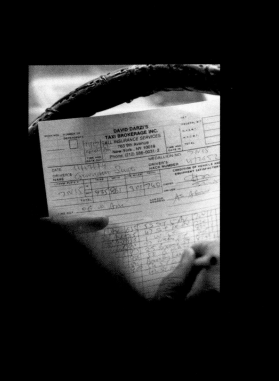

OLD PEOPLE, THEY LIKE TO GET TO THE AIRPORT EARLY.

DEMOCRACY IS ONLY BECAUSE EVERYONE WANTS OTHERS TO SHARE THE BLAME.

REGULAR AIR IS SWEETER THAN AIR CONDITIONING.

WHOMEVER IS IN POWER IS NOT IN TROUBLE.

MARRIAGE IS FOR WHEN YOU LIFE IS NOT SO GOOD.

YOU CAN'T PROMISE PEOPLE NOTHING BECAUSE THERE'S ALWAYS SOMETHING IN THE TUNNEL.

TIME GOES.
THAT'S IT.

LEASE SIT BA
IN CASE OF
SHORT STOP
OR YOUR OWN SAFE

PEOPLE ARE SCARED OF PEOPLE HERE WHILE I'M NOT EVEN SCARED OF A TIGER.

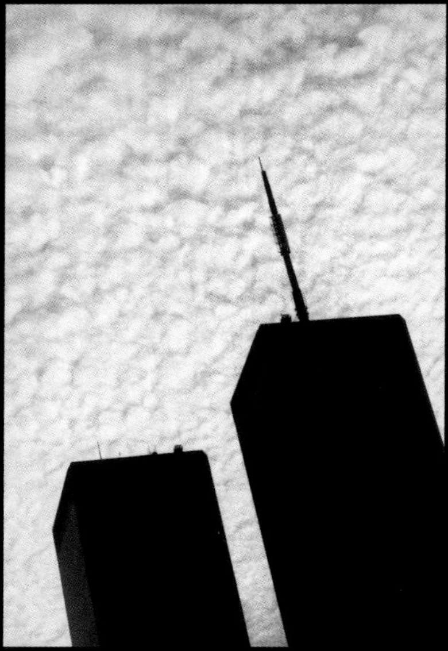

WOMEN CHOOSE WHO THEY LOVE THE MOST. MEN CHOOSE WHO LOVES THEM THE MOST.

WHATEVER YOU BECOME, SOMEONE WILL LONG FOR WHAT YOU WERE.

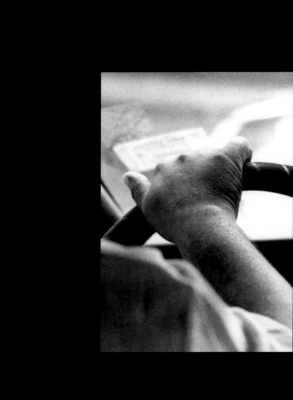

HE THE BIG FISH, I THE SMALL FISH.

THERE'S NO NEED TO STAND BEHIND ANYONE WHEN THERE'S SO MUCH ROOM TO WALK.

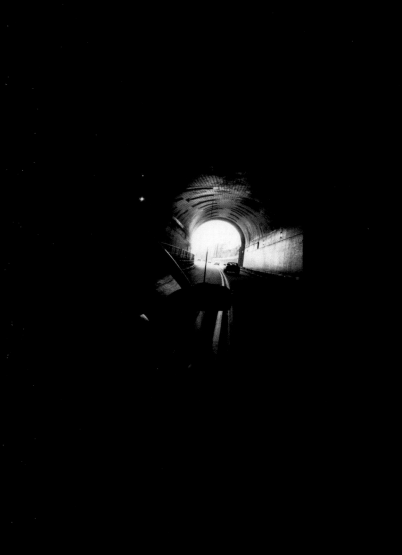

DEATH IS AN END AND A BEGINNING.

on checking yourself
out in rearview mirrors

IF YOUR DRIVER HAVE NOTHING INTERESTING TO SAY TO YOU, MAYBE BECAUSE YOU HAVE NOTHING INTERESTING TO SAY TO HIM.

ADDITIONAL ACKNOWLEDGMENTS

Caroline Herter, Emily Miller, Michael Ash, Zach Shiskall, Sarah Malarkey, Marcia Lippman, Ben Roghtfeld, Patrick O'Hara, Felicia Stingone, Jeff Stone, Alison Seiffer, Kirshenbaum & Bond, Ludovic Moulin, George, Marie, George, and Annette Dugan, Ira, Yvette, And Julia Mickenberg, my amazing grandparents, Brian Randall, Carre Bevilaqua, Martin Pederson, Serge Shea, Darac, Ella Booth, Bea, Bob, Pam, and Melia Hughes, Anna Blinken. Thanks for your generous help and guidance on this book. And, thank you Steve Kessler.

A PORTION OF THE PROCEEDS OF THIS BOOK WILL GO TOWARD REALLY BIG TIPS.

VEHICLE OPER
NEW YORK CITY TAXI and

EXPIRES

LAST DAY OF

FEE

FRIEI

1

FRIEDR
NIETZSC